Building a Solitaire Game and a Peg Board

Ken Ainsworth

Illustrations by Tina Holdcroft
Photography by Rodrigo Moreno

Annick Press • Toronto • New York • Vancouver

THE CANADA COUNCIL | LE CONSEIL DES ARTS
FOR THE ARTS | DU CANADA
SINCE 1957 | DEPUIS 1957

We acknowledge the support of the Canada Council for the Arts
for our publishing program. We also thank the Ontario Arts Council.

Cataloguing in Publication Data
Ainsworth, Ken, 1957-
        Building a solitaire game and a peg board

(Building together ; 1)
ISBN 1-55037-554-7 (bound) ISBN 1-55037-512-1 (pbk.)

1. Woodwork – Juvenile literature. 2. Games – Design and construction –
Juvenile literature. I. Holdcroft, Tina. II. Moreno, Rodrigo. III. Title.
IV. Series: Ainsworth, Ken, 1957–   . Building together ; 1.

TT185.A363 1998   j684'.08   C98-931294-1

The art in this book was rendered in watercolours.
The text was typeset in Times Roman and Officina Sans.

Distributed in Canada by:
Firefly Books Ltd.
3680 Victoria Park Avenue
Willowdale, ON
M2H 3K1

Published in the U.S.A. by Annick Press (U.S.) Ltd.
Distributed in the U.S.A. by:
Firefly Books (U.S.) Inc.
P.O. Box 1338
Ellicott Station
Buffalo, NY 14205

Printed and bound in Canada by Friesens.

Introduction

In the spring of 1994, my daughters and I gathered up some scrap wood and a few basic hand tools. I thought we'd see what we could come up with.

The flower Lindsey made sits beside Carly's "person" on my desk, and both have "Made in Childhood" stamped all over them—only a child could have worked the gleeful inexactness and the wonderfully rough cutting job. My daughters' joy in their work and our memories of building together provided the seedling from which the concept of this series grew.

These books aren't about making perfect objects from wood, or turning children into skilled woodworkers. They are about adults—with or without woodworking training—and children having fun together. My training actually got in the way at first. I had to learn that children are justifiably proud of work that to me still looks a bit rough, but now I love that mark of authenticity.

This is not to say that we adults can't sometimes step in and say, "Do you mind if I sand this a bit more?" Just don't take a power sander and grind away all the marks of the child's work. Sometimes it will be necessary to finish, or even do, some task that the child finds frustrating or too difficult. Even then, I try to keep in mind that it's the child's project and he or she needs to give permission before I can mess with it.

Before you start, it is important that you read the safety guidelines on page 4 and discuss them with the child you'll be working with.

The *Building Together* series is designed to be easy to follow for both adults and kids. Every photograph shows exactly how Lindsey and I did that step, and the instructions are like listening to our conversation as we worked. Sidebars give details about the skills needed for the steps on each page. (Note: We worked with hand tools for this series, since they are safer than power tools, readily available, relatively inexpensive, and satisfying to use.) Each book provides a miniature woodworking course, but feel free to do whichever projects you like—each one is self-contained. Most of all, have fun building together!

Ken Ainsworth

Contents

Page **5**

Page **13**

Safety

There is, of course, some risk involved in working with tools. Working safely is twofold: taking precautions to minimize risk and being careful while we are working.

Preparing the work area

Remember that children have not yet reached adult levels of co-ordination. They move differently, they are less cautious, and have sudden bursts of restless energy. With these things in mind:

● Store spare lumber well away from the work area. Leaning boards against the wall is okay as long as they are not too long or wobbly. Alternatively, lay them on the floor against the wall.

● Put away sharp tools as soon as you are finished using them. Never leave tools, pieces of wood, or other equipment lying around on tables, chairs, benches or floors, where people can step on them, trip over them or stumble against them.

● Whatever you decide to use as your "workbench" (see Tools and Materials, page 6), make sure that it is sturdy and won't collapse or tip over.

● Keep a bag of small wood scraps on hand for using as saw blocks, cutting guides, and clamp pads. (For more information, see the Tools and Materials pages and sidebars on clamping.)

● Keep out small children and pets! You can't supervise the older child's woodworking and watch over a young child at the same time. A playful dog or cat can knock things over, jump onto work surfaces, and cause harm to materials, people, and themselves.

Things to watch out for while working

Irritation and fatigue can greatly increase the risk of accidents. Be sure to take your time, set reasonable goals, limit the length of each session, and take frequent breaks when building together, especially if someone small *or* big gets frustrated or angry.

Children must always be supervised when woodworking, and both adults and children must follow some basic rules.

● Always wear safety glasses when you are sawing or hammering, or any time when little or big things might fly around and get into or near eyes.

● Wear dust masks to help keep sawdust and woodchips out of mouths and noses.

● Younger children should hold tools such as saws and hammers in both hands for added strength and control, and so that one hand doesn't get in harm's way. (See sidebars for more information.)

● Even sandpaper can cause injury. It tends to sand skin as well as wood, and the paper can pick up splinters, which then get stuck in fingers and hands.

● Children should never be allowed to run or jump around the work area.

● Both children and adults must wear sturdy footwear with thick uppers.

We all learn by making mistakes. The adult's job is doing everything possible to see that the learning process doesn't result in injury.

Solitaire Game

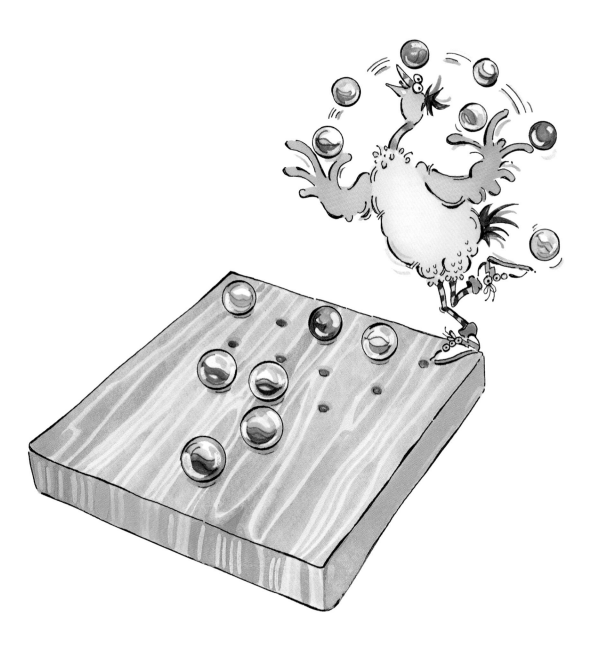

Tools and Materials

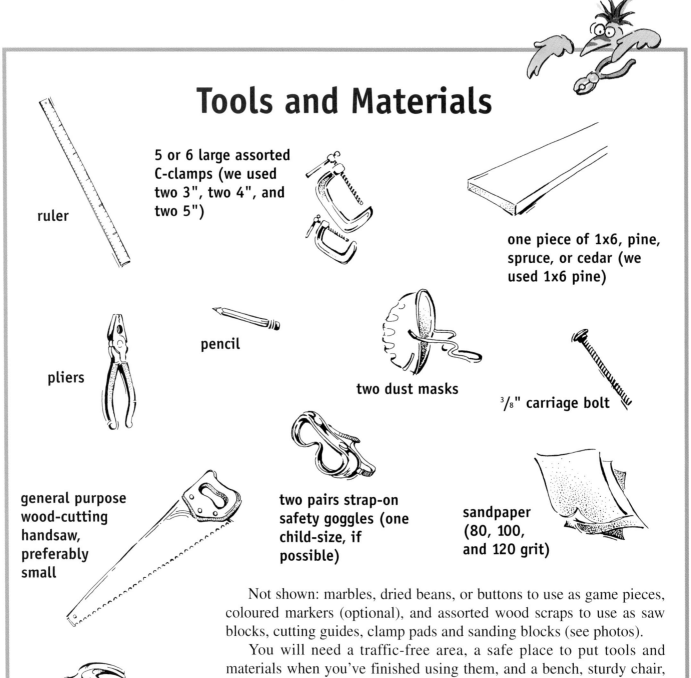

ruler

5 or 6 large assorted C-clamps (we used two 3", two 4", and two 5")

one piece of 1x6, pine, spruce, or cedar (we used 1x6 pine)

pencil

pliers

two dust masks

$^{3}/_{8}$" carriage bolt

general purpose wood-cutting handsaw, preferably small

two pairs strap-on safety goggles (one child-size, if possible)

sandpaper (80, 100, and 120 grit)

child's hammer (though a big one will do)

Not shown: marbles, dried beans, or buttons to use as game pieces, coloured markers (optional), and assorted wood scraps to use as saw blocks, cutting guides, clamp pads and sanding blocks (see photos).

You will need a traffic-free area, a safe place to put tools and materials when you've finished using them, and a bench, sturdy chair, picnic table, edge of a deck, or other suitable surface. If you are working with long boards, add another support of a similar height (see photos for peg board project).

Most lumberyards use the imperial system of measurement. If you want to use metric, convert our measurements, counting 2.54 centimetres per inch.

Illustrations not to scale

Names for tools can vary. If you are unsure about terms, ask at your local hardware store or lumberyard.

When Lindsey came home from her friend Rachel's house she asked, "Dad, can we make a game with a piece of the wood that's left over from building our fence?"

"Sure. What kind of game?"

"Well, it's made from a piece of flat wood, like this." She held up her hands. "It will be square. We'll put holes in it for marbles, and then one marble can jump over another one. You keep going like that until only one is left. Rachel has one."

"I think it's called solitaire," Dad said. "I'll help you cut the wood and make the holes."

"Great!"

About wood

Boards are called "one by six", "two by four", etc. We also write this 1x6, 2x4, etc. This refers to the size the board was when it was cut from the log. Smoothing and trimming makes it slightly smaller.

Clamping

Clamp the 1x6 to the work surface as shown, using wood scraps as pads to protect the boards from damage by the clamps. Longer boards need support: rest each end on surfaces of similar height, clamping the second support if desired.

Then clamp on the cutting guide and the saw block. The cutting guide lies across the end of the 1x6. The saw block lies alongside it, *extending past the cutting line*. This will stop the saw when the cut is done. Clamp everything firmly.

1

"Exactly how big would you like this game to be?" Dad asked. Lindsey showed him. "About six by six inches," he said. Lindsey measured six inches from one end of the one by six. She measured along one edge, then the other, and drew a line connecting the marks.

2

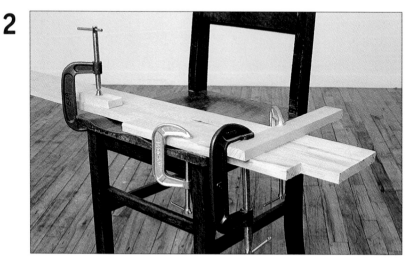

"I'll make you a saw block and a cutting guide," Dad said. First he clamped the one by six to the two chairs (see photo next page). Then he clamped a piece of scrap wood beside the board to block the saw once Lindsey was finished cutting. Lastly he clamped a piece of scrap along the cutting line.

3

"Okay, Lindsey, I'll start the cut and you can finish it."
Lindsey had trouble getting the saw to move easily, so
Dad stood behind her, reached around and helped keep
the saw moving.

"Good job," he said when they were done.

4

Dad showed Lindsey how to sand the wood to make it
smooth. "It's easiest if you sand in the direction of the
grain." Lindsey sanded until there were no splinters or
really rough spots left.

Sawing

A handsaw cuts when it is
being pushed down. To
begin a cut, place the teeth
along the outside of the
cutting line. Drag the saw
back to make a shallow
groove, then push to begin
cutting. Younger children
often find it easier to hold
the saw with both hands.
Lindsey is using one hand
with Dad's help and keep-
ing her free hand well
away from the blade. For
more on sawing, see p. 19.

Sanding

Sandpaper comes in vari-
ous "grits": 50 for rough
sanding, 220 for very fine,
and several in between.
Lindsey started with 80
grit, then went to 100. For
making a sanding block,
see p. 11.

Drawing the grid

Draw a straight line along one side of the game board, about ¾" from the edge. Draw another line next to it about ½" from the first one. Repeat until you have nine lines. Then turn the board sideways. Repeat, this time with lines 1" apart, until you have five lines.

Now draw the circles as in the pattern below, spacing them 1" apart.

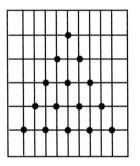

Rules

Set up the game by placing marbles in each of the holes except the one at the tip. The goal of the game is to have only one marble left. A marble can be removed only after jumping another marble over it.

5

"Where should the holes go?"

"Rachel's has a triangle with five holes on each side. The holes need to be far enough apart so we can pick up the marbles." Lindsey got a marble and held it so Dad could measure. Then she used a ruler to draw a grid.

6

The lines of the grid showed Lindsey how far apart the holes had to be. She followed the grid pattern of Rachel's game (see sidebar) to draw little circles where she and Dad would make the holes.

7

Dad said, "Now we need to make the holes. I'll hold the bolt with the pliers so that it will be straight and won't move, and you tap it with your hammer for each hole."

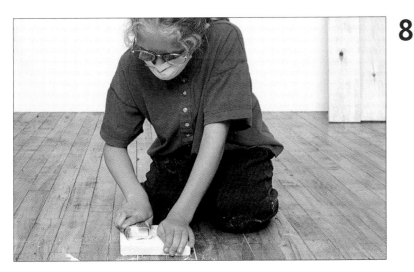

8

Then Lindsey did a little touch-up sanding around the edges of holes, wiped away the sawdust, and decorated the board with markers. The solitaire game was done.

(If you would like to use a finish, follow the instructions on the can.)

Hammering

The adult should hold the carriage bolt upright with pliers. Children often have better control when holding the hammer with both hands.

Sanding

Use 120 grit to get rid of any rough edges, splinters, or unwanted marks. It is best to use an eraser for the pencil lines. Remember to sand "with the grain", which means in the same direction as the lines in the wood.

To make a sanding block, choose a piece of wood that fits easily in your hand. Wrap the block in a quarter sheet of sandpaper. The block makes the paper easier to use, and helps in sanding evenly because it keeps the paper flat.

"How do you play this game?" asked Dad.

"You put marbles in all the holes except the one at the very tip. Then you jump over marbles, and each one you jump over you take away, until only one is left. I'll get some marbles and show you."

Lindsey played the game and had two marbles left. Dad tried and had three left.

"Don't worry, Dad. If you keep practising, you'll get better at it. Thanks for helping me make it."

"You're very welcome."

Lindsey went to show Mom her new game.

Peg Board

Tools and Materials

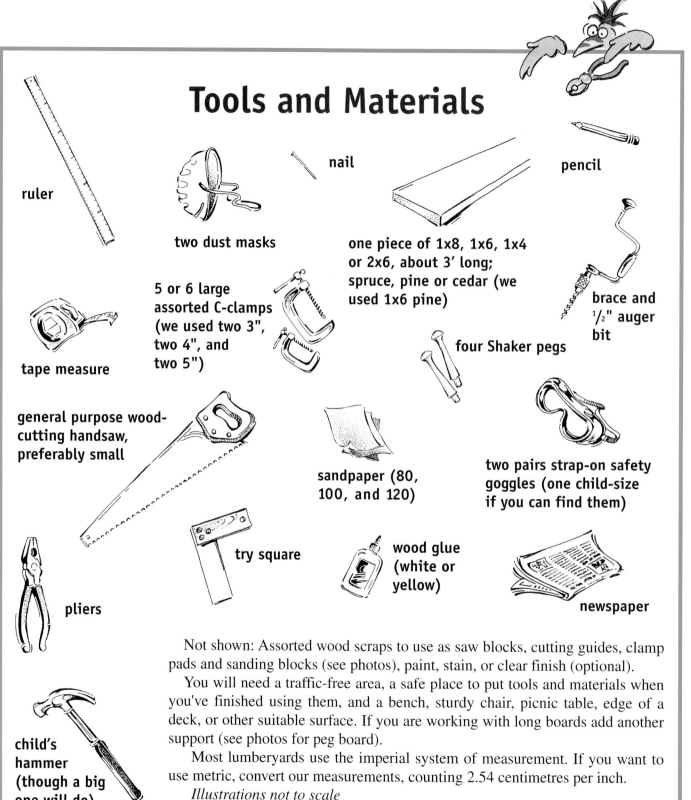

ruler

two dust masks

nail

one piece of 1x8, 1x6, 1x4 or 2x6, about 3' long; spruce, pine or cedar (we used 1x6 pine)

pencil

brace and 1/2" auger bit

tape measure

5 or 6 large assorted C-clamps (we used two 3", two 4", and two 5")

four Shaker pegs

general purpose wood-cutting handsaw, preferably small

sandpaper (80, 100, and 120)

two pairs strap-on safety goggles (one child-size if you can find them)

try square

wood glue (white or yellow)

newspaper

pliers

child's hammer (though a big one will do)

Not shown: Assorted wood scraps to use as saw blocks, cutting guides, clamp pads and sanding blocks (see photos), paint, stain, or clear finish (optional).

You will need a traffic-free area, a safe place to put tools and materials when you've finished using them, and a bench, sturdy chair, picnic table, edge of a deck, or other suitable surface. If you are working with long boards add another support (see photos for peg board).

Most lumberyards use the imperial system of measurement. If you want to use metric, convert our measurements, counting 2.54 centimetres per inch.

Illustrations not to scale

Names for tools can vary. If you are unsure about terms, ask at your local hardware store or lumberyard.

Dad was playing Lindsey's solitaire game at the kitchen table one day when she came in from outside and hung her jacket over a chair.

"Dad, the closet's full again," she said.

"How about if we make a board with pegs sticking out to hang your jackets on? We could put it there beside the door."

"Okay."

Dad got out some scrap paper and made a sketch of the peg board.

About Wood

Boards are called "one by six", "two by four", etc. We also write this 1x6, 2x4, etc. This refers to the size the board was when it was cut from the log. Smoothing and trimming makes it slightly smaller.

Checking for square

Hold the square against the end of the board. If there is a gap between the blade of the square and the edge of the wood, the end isn't square.

If the gap is wide, make a new cut to correct the angle. Use the try square to draw a new cutting line about 2" from the end of the 1x6. That's enough wood to support the saw while you're cutting.

If the gap is small, you can correct it by sanding (see p. 20).

1

Dad and Lindsey got their board from the garage. Dad said, "We'll have to check the end to see if it's square." Lindsey took his try square and fitted it around the corner of the board. They could see a big gap between the board and the blade. "We'll cut it straight," said Dad.

2

"We'll have to cut about two inches off the end to make it straight." Lindsey measured the two inches with a ruler, and used the square to draw a cutting line across the end of the board.

SHAKER PEG BOARD

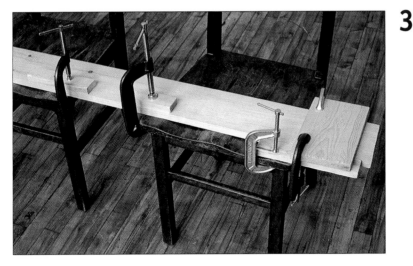

3

Dad clamped the one by six to two chairs, making sure the cutting line was well past the edge. They used two chairs because the board was long and needed support at both ends. He also clamped on a cutting guide and a saw block to help Lindsey.

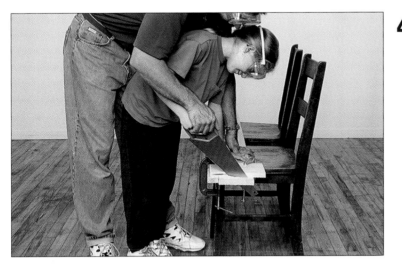

4

Dad put the saw on the outside of the cutting line and started the cut. He sawed about halfway through the one by six, steadying the board with his left hand. Then Lindsey did the rest, with a little help from him.

Clamping

Clamp the 1x6 to the work surface as shown, using wood scraps as pads to protect the boards from damage by the clamps. Longer boards need support: rest each end on surfaces of similar height, clamping the second support if desired.

Now clamp the cutting guide and the saw block. The cutting guide lies across the end of the 1x6. The saw block lies beside it, *extending past the cutting line*. This will stop the saw when the cut is done. Clamp everything firmly.

Sawing

A handsaw cuts when it is pushed down. To begin a cut, place the teeth along the outside of the cutting line. Drag the saw back to make a shallow groove, then push to begin cutting. Younger children often find it easier to hold the saw with both hands. Lindsey is using one hand with Dad's help and keeping her free hand well away from the blade. For more on sawing, see p. 19.

SHAKER PEG BOARD

Checking for square tip

Remember to hold the try square firmly against the edge of the board.

Safety tip

If your bench or chair is sliding on the floor, try bracing it against a wall. Placing the legs on pieces of thin foam rubber can also work well.

Sawing tip

Holding the saw with both hands can give the younger woodworker more strength and better control.

5

Lindsey took the clamps off and checked the new cut to make sure it was square. "It looks fine, I think," she said.

"Great," Dad said. "Now we need to mark how long it will be."

6

Dad gave her his tape measure. She measured two feet from the newly cut end of the board, and made a pencil mark. Then, using the try square, she drew a line from that mark across to the other side of the board.

SHAKER PEG BOARD

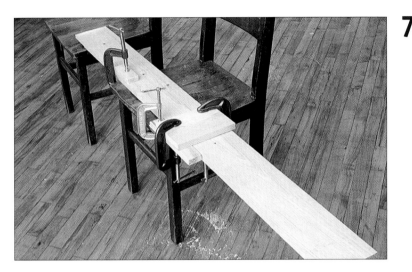

7

Lindsey clamped the one by six to the chair. Then she clamped the cutting guide and the saw block. Dad did the last bit of tightening for her.

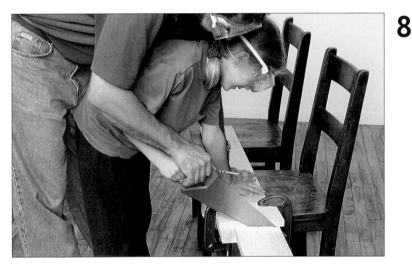

8

Dad helped Lindsey with the sawing. When they finished, Dad said, "Good job, Lindsey. Why don't we take a break?"

Clamping tip

If you're using a board much longer than ours, you might want to rest the "free" end on a third support, or ask someone to hold it.

Sawing tips

Sawing is hard work. It's a good idea for an adult to begin the cut and let the child finish. If the child is having difficulty, do the sawing together.

Try to cut with smooth, even strokes, keeping the saw going along the cutting line. Try not to let the saw lean to one side.

Bracing your free hand against the board steadies the work surface, gives you added leverage, and keeps the hand out of trouble.

SHAKER PEG BOARD

Sanding

Sandpaper comes in various "grits": 50 for rough sanding, 220 for very fine and more in between.

Sanding for square

Sanding is an easy way to straighten a slightly crooked cut. For squaring the end of a board, 50 or 80 grit sandpaper would work well. To avoid rounding the end, use a sanding block.

Many different types of sanding blocks are available in stores, but you can also make your own.

Making a sanding block

To make a sanding block, choose a piece of wood that fits easily in your hand. Wrap it in a quarter sheet of sandpaper. The block makes the paper easier to use, and helps in sanding evenly because it keeps the paper flat.

9

When they came back, Dad said, "Let's see how straight your cut is." Lindsey took the try square and checked the newly cut end. "Hey, that's a really good cut. Look, it's almost perfect," Dad said.

10

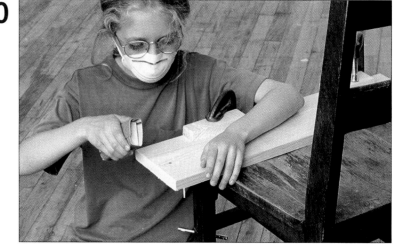

Since the cut was so good, the only thing needed to make it perfectly square was a bit of sanding. Lindsey took a sanding block and began working on the one by six where it wasn't quite 90°. Every now and then she checked it with the try square.

11

When Lindsey was satisfied that the new cut was square, she and Dad took turns sanding the whole piece of one by six until it felt fairly smooth. They rounded the corners a bit too.

12

"We're going to measure the holes for the pegs now, right?" Lindsey asked.

"That's right." Lindsey figured out how wide the board was and drew a line down the middle of it lengthwise. Then she marked the places for the holes.

Sanding for smoothness

Sanding is done in steps, beginning with a coarse grit and moving to a finer one. When you are sanding the completed project, a sequence of 80, 100, and 120 will be fine. Get all of the imperfections out with 80 grit and then use 100 and 120 to make the wood smoother.

Sand in the direction of the "grain" (the lines you see on the surface of the wood), except when you work on the end of a board, where there are no grain lines.

Measuring for peg holes

Begin by drawing a straight line, centred between the edges, from one end of the board to the other. Space the marks for the holes evenly along this line.

SHAKER PEG BOARD

Hammering

The adult should hold the nail upright with pliers. Children often have better control when holding the hammer with both hands.

Clamping

Clamp the board to two supports (see right).

Inserting a bit

The end of a brace that holds the bit is called a "chuck". It has "fingers" that open and close when the chuck is held still while you're turning the brace. These fingers hold the bit. Close the fingers slightly so the bit just fits in between them. Insert the bit fully, then hold the chuck and crank the brace to tighten the fingers.

Drilling

Place the point of the drill bit where each hole is to be made and keep the brace upright by holding the top handle. Turn the crank clockwise to begin drilling.

13

"It will be easier to drill if we make little holes with a nail first," Dad said. Using the pliers, he held a nail on each of Lindsey's pencil marks. She tapped the nail with the hammer, and they had a tiny hole where each of the pegs would go.

14

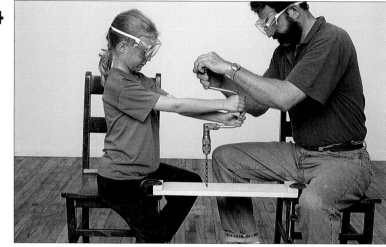

Dad put a half-inch bit in the brace. Then he clamped each end of the board to a chair. He and Lindsey sat facing each other. Dad placed the bit in the first hole, and held the brace upright and steady while Lindsey cranked. She stopped when the bit started to poke through.

15

"Now you can glue the pegs in," said Dad. Lindsey put a bit of glue into the first hole and then slipped a peg in, holding it upright and pressing down gently. She kept going until all four pegs were in.

16

"We have to tap the pegs so they'll go all the way into the holes," Dad said. He held a piece of scrap wood on the end of the pegs to protect them from the hammer.

"Good job!" he said. "We'll leave this for a few hours so the glue can set."

Gluing

Wipe away any sawdust with a clean cloth before gluing the pegs.

The pegs need enough glue to hold them in place, but not so much that glue squeezes out around the peg when it's inserted. Squeeze three or four drops of glue at different points on the inside lip of the hole so that the glue runs down into it. Wipe off the excess glue with a damp cloth.

Tip

Surfaces to be glued together need to fit well, with few or no gaps. Glue will hold tight joints with a strength equal to that of the wood itself, but does not work as a gap filler.

Tapping the pegs

The pegs should fit tightly enough in the holes that light tapping with a hammer is necessary to get them all the way in. This gives them more support.

A few days later, Dad was playing solitaire at the kitchen table again when Lindsey came in and hung her jacket on a chair.

"Lindsey, why aren't you using the peg board?"

Then he noticed that all the pegs on the board were being used to hang two backpacks, his umbrella, Lindsey's rain jacket and a stuffed snake. "I see…."

He laughed, got up and put his backpack and umbrella in the closet.